D1252636

The United States: Historical Atlases of the Growth of a New Nation ™

A HISTORICAL ATLAS OF

# The Industrial Age and the Growth of America's Cities

## Sherri Liberman

The Rosen Publishing Group, Inc., New York

*For Michael, always*
*"To laugh often and love much . . . to appreciate beauty, to find the best in others, to give one's self . . . this is to have succeeded." — Ralph Waldo Emerson*

Published in 2005 by The Rosen Publishing Group, Inc.
29 East 21st Street, New York, NY 10010

First Edition

**Library of Congress Cataloging-in-Publication Data**

Liberman, Sherri.
A historical atlas of the industrial age and the growth of America's cities/by Sherri Liberman.—1st ed.
     p. cm.—(The United States, historical atlases of the growth of a new nation)
Includes bibliographical references and index.
ISBN 1-4042-0205-6 (library binding)
1. Industrial revolution—United States—Juvenile literature. 2. Cities and towns—United States—Growth—History—Juvenile literature. 3. Industrial revolution—United States—Maps for children. 4. Cities and towns—United States—Growth—History—Maps for children.
I. Title. II. Series.
HC105.L525 2005
330.973'08—dc22

                                                                                    2004002742

*Manufactured in the United States of America*

**On the cover:** Top: American inventor Thomas Alva Edison. Bottom: A bird's-eye view of New York City in 1883. Background: A nineteenth-century image of the United States that features several Pacific rail lines.

# Contents

# INTRODUCTION

The United States began its rise as an industrialized nation after the Civil War ended in 1865 and continued to develop until the beginning of World War I in 1917. The success of the farming, mining, and cattle industries attracted explorers to the American frontier. More United States territory was settled in the late 1800s than in the first 250 years, when the British colonies existed only on its eastern coast. Much of the West joined the Union during this time, including California (1850), Nevada (1864), Colorado (1876), Washington (1889), Wyoming (1890), and New Mexico and Arizona (1912). However, settlement of the frontier came with a price. Brutal confrontations occurred between American

Transportation connections between Southern cities can be seen on this map of the United States, created during the Civil War (1861–1865). New methods of transportation and communication, such as the railroad and telegraph, were crucial to both the Union (North) and Confederate (South) armies during the conflict. Transportation by rail helped move soldiers and their supplies. News of the war was communicated by telegraph swiftly and without misinterpretation. Just as easily, however, both sides were able to block railroads to Northern and Southern points, slowing shipping or stopping it altogether.

settlers who took land from Native American tribes who had dwelled there for ages.

During the 1870s, America moved into a decade known as the Gilded Age, a term that emerged from written works of the period. The nation shifted from an agricultural to an industrial economy. Industries such as petroleum refining, steel manufacturing, and electrical power emerged. Americans also witnessed the creation of a transcontinental railroad. Hard economic times sent many farmers from rural America into cities in search of work.

The industrial economy also transformed America's social structure. A new class of wealthy industrialists, an upcoming middle class, and an expanded working class emerged. The labor force developed from masses of immigrants, as well as from relocated farmers. Soon, harsh working conditions, unemployment, and low wages influenced the creation of the nation's first organized labor movement.

The Gilded Age produced inventions such as the lightbulb and the telephone, making life easier. However, it was still a hazardous time. Overcrowding, crime, and violence were commonplace. Women demanded voting (suffrage) rights, and reformers protested to reduce child labor.

The Industrial Revolution radically altered the way Americans lived. Cities that were now illuminated in electric light and built high with skyscrapers offered an exciting alternative to rural life. Suburbs evolved with the invention of the electric trolley, the underground subway, and, finally, the automobile. These innovations in transportation connected families to their city jobs with progressively more speed and ease.

Progress made during the Industrial Revolution influenced the growth of the United States, ultimately making it the powerful and wealthy country that it is today.

# CHAPTER ONE
## The Promise of the West

President Abraham Lincoln once described the American West as the "treasure of the nation." Its lure of gold and silver deposits convinced countless settlers to venture west of the Mississippi River in search of wealth.

The gold rush began in 1848 when John Marshall discovered gold at a sawmill in California. A flood of prospectors who abandoned their former livelihoods for a chance at discovering gold soon followed. Once they arrived in California, most found scores of competing miners instead of riches. More than 90,000 "forty-niners," as they were called, made the difficult cross-country journey to California by foot or covered wagon.

The gold rush changed the political landscape of California, which joined the Union in 1850 shortly after gold was discovered. But California was not prepared to govern effectively in the midst of the gold rush. There was little order during this time, and no military force. California was not divided and settled, and no government officials collected taxes.

When silver deposits were discovered at the Comstock Lode in Virginia City, Nevada, in 1859, many miners left California in search of silver. But mining for silver was more expensive and complicated than mining for gold. Successful silver mining required organized work crews, wealthy investors, and mining companies.

In 1861, the Civil War broke out. President Lincoln opposed slavery in the western territories. Starting in 1860, seven Southern states seceded from the Union to form the Confederate States of America. As the bloodiest war in U.S. history, the Civil War took as many lives as all other U.S. conflicts combined.

Nevada and California played key financial roles in ending the Civil War. Lincoln took advantage of the economic boom in the West to lure Nevada into joining the Union in 1864. With Nevada's contribution of $45 million to the federal government, along with gold profits from California, these states contributed to the defeat of the Confederacy in 1865.

## Railroad Expansion

The railroads that linked the coasts of the United States symbolized the age of industrial capitalism in America. The steel, coal, and iron industries developed out of the material needs of railroads. Towns soon sprang up along the miles of tracks being laid. The growth of cities was made possible by the ability of freight cars to transport large supplies of food and fuel across longer distances. Agriculture also expanded because of the railroads. Farmers now had the ability to ship large quantities of produce, cattle, and grain to distant cities.

Since 1832, the United States had recognized a need to link California to the rest of the country through a coast-to-coast railroad system. However, it wasn't until 1862 that Congress passed the Pacific Railway Act. This law authorized the building of the nation's first transcontinental railroad. The Union Pacific Railroad laid track west from Omaha,

This nineteenth-century engraving depicts a typical mining camp during the gold rush of 1848 to 1849. As many as 80,000 miners traveled west to California in 1849 after news spread about the findings of gold. After snow blocked traditional trails during the winter of 1848 to 1849, miners were so desperate to travel west that many booked passages on steamships. Because of this push to migrate, San Francisco soon became the third most important port in the nation behind New York and Boston.

Nebraska, and the Central Pacific Railroad built east from Sacramento, California. Although the Civil War slowed its construction, by 1866, investment in the project increased. In 1869, the two lines met at Promontory Summit in Utah.

In the decades that followed the Civil War, railroad construction led to economic growth. The settlement of the frontier expanded agriculture, and the exploitation of natural resources led to the demand for a faster way to move goods across longer distances. Since shippers were dependent on the railroads to transport products, some railroads engaged in corrupt business practices such as price-fixing. Price-fixing occurs when two competing companies agree to set the price of a service at a certain rate. Price-fixing discourages competition. Shippers and passengers located in small-town regions, where there was little competition, were often subjected to the unfair practices of railroad monopolies. The railroads often provided discounts only to large shippers or buyers. Many American farmers in the South and West, called Grangers, lacked the shipment volume to obtain the more competitive rates. The Granger political movement was formed in the 1860s to provide more benefits to these isolated rural communities.

In addition, building railroads was a backbreaking business that fewer and fewer people wanted to do. To solve the labor problem, about 15,000 Chinese immigrants were recruited by California governor Leland Stanford to work on the Central Pacific Railroad.

Although rail lines crossed the United States by the 1880s, there was still a need to streamline the rail system. The development of standard gauge rails in the 1880s made the interconnection of all routes possible by applying a uniform space between each rail for all lines.

Timing was another important factor in standardizing the railroads. Before the invention of railroads, clocks were set to local time, where noon would occur when the sun was at its highest point. But train routes that occurred across long distances needed to be synchronized. The need to coordinate rail schedules led to the adoption of four standardized time zones in the United States and Canada in 1883. This system was soon adopted internationally, and the world was divided into twenty-four time zones.

## Native American Policy

The expansion of the southwestern United States further aggravated the federal government's relationship with Native Americans. This

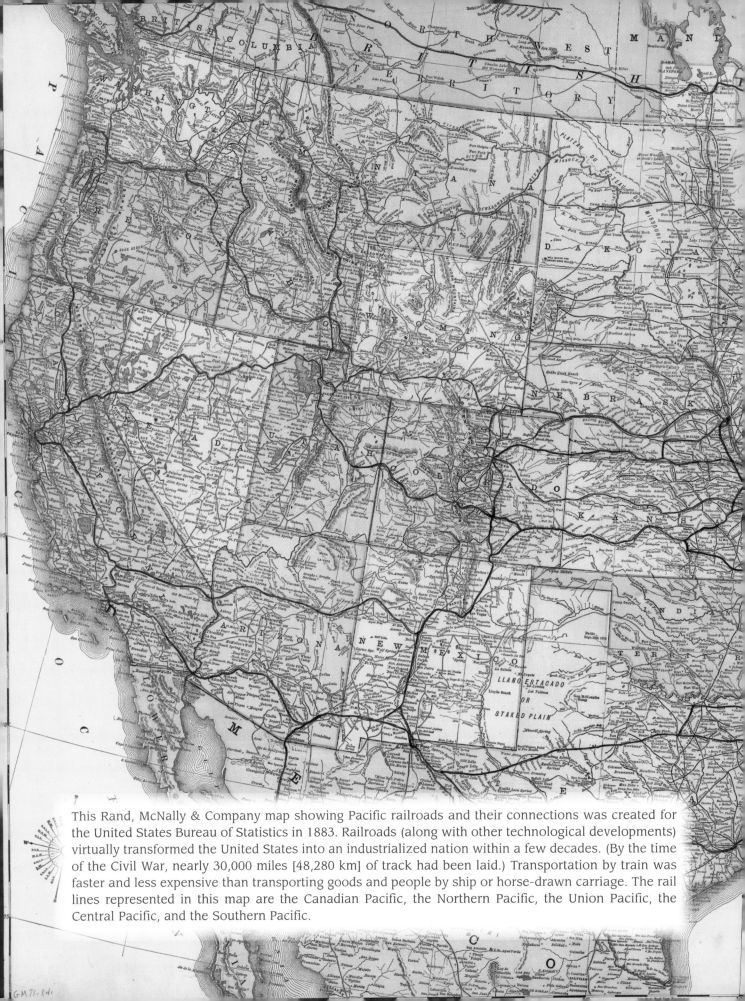

This Rand, McNally & Company map showing Pacific railroads and their connections was created for the United States Bureau of Statistics in 1883. Railroads (along with other technological developments) virtually transformed the United States into an industrialized nation within a few decades. (By the time of the Civil War, nearly 30,000 miles [48,280 km] of track had been laid.) Transportation by train was faster and less expensive than transporting goods and people by ship or horse-drawn carriage. The rail lines represented in this map are the Canadian Pacific, the Northern Pacific, the Union Pacific, the Central Pacific, and the Southern Pacific.

MAP

EXHIBITING THE SEVERAL

PACIFIC RAILROADS

PREPARED FOR THE REPORT

ON THE

INTERNAL COMMERCE OF THE UNITED STATES

BY THE

CHIEF OF THE BUREAU OF STATISTICS.

RAND, McNALLY & CO.

1883.

EXPLANATION:

___ Lines...........

___ and connecting Lines...........

# Chinese Railroad Workers

Chinese laborers were trained to blast and move rocks, clear mountainous land, and lay railroad ties. Many workers were killed as tracks were built into the high Sierra Nevada mountains. Workers suffered from the effects of intense heat and cold, often working six days a week. Explosions from dynamite often led to accidental injuries and deaths. The Chinese were making about $26 a month for their labor, compared to $36 a month for their white counterparts.

When the railway was completed in 1869, the Chinese were excluded from the opening ceremonies and were not acknowledged for their participation in its construction. When the Chinese attempted to settle inland, they were constantly harassed and threatened, and they were often chased out of town. Then, in the 1880s, the Chinese were recruited again. This time, they worked on the Southern Pacific Railroad, which connected all the states in the Union. Again, conditions were harsh in the Arizona desert, and the Chinese were the only people who would work.

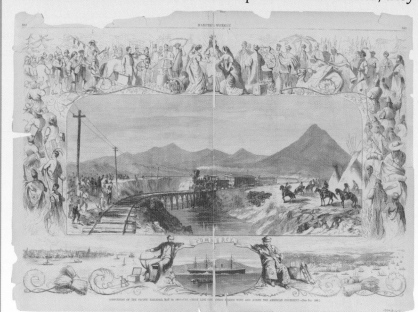

This illustration of Chinese immigrants was featured in *Harper's Weekly* in 1869 to coincide with the completion of the Pacific Railroad on May 10 of that same year. Without other means of employment, many Chinese opted for the dangerous work of clearing land. According to Judge E. B. Crocker, who offered legal counsel to the Central Pacific, the Chinese were "far more reliable [than whites, especially because there was] No danger of strike among them." In the end, about 12,000 Chinese had been on the Central Pacific's payroll.

conflict was commonly referred to as the Native American "problem."

With the annexation of Texas (1845), the acquisition of the territory that became Arizona and New Mexico (the Gadsden Purchase of 1854), and the end of the Mexican-American War (1848), more settlers migrated to the Southwest. The Americans continually felt it was their mission to "liberate" the land from Native Americans for the country's agricultural needs. They viewed the Native American lifestyle of using the land for hunting and gathering as wasteful and primitive. The government applied land policies that nearly destroyed Native American lifestyles.

The federal government decided to solve this problem by relocating Indians to reservations. Beginning around 1850, reservations were supposed to protect Native Americans from white invasions. At the same time, the reservations restrained Indians from harassing prospectors and fighting with neighboring tribes. The motivation behind this plan was the desire to take Indian land. If the Native Americans who moved to these reservations adopted an agricultural lifestyle, the government would provide them with agricultural tools. These goods were offered if the Indians adopted American-style clothing and housing. Several tribes relocated, and in the process, signed government treaties.

Around 1870, constant invasions from prospectors, cattlemen, and farmers, arriving via the transcontinental railroad, resulted in the

uncommitted to any other course than the strict line of constitutional duty; and that the securities for this independence may be rendered as strong as the nature of power and the weakness of its possessor will admit, — I cannot too earnestly invite your attention to the propriety of promoting such an amendment of the constitution as will render him ineligible after one term of service.

It gives me pleasure to announce to Congress that the benevolent policy of the Government, steadily pursued for nearly thirty years in relation to the removal

Native Americans, called "savages" in this document written in the hand of President Andrew Jackson, were expected to migrate to specific settlements chosen by the federal government. With the ongoing pressure of pioneers to move farther west in the spirit of Manifest Destiny, Jackson justified his policy of Indian removal in this message that was delivered to Congress on December 6, 1830. Jackson called his policy "advantageous" to Native Americans since they were able to, "cast off their savage habits and become an interesting, civilized, and Christian community."

outbreak of brutal wars with Native Americans. The U.S. government continued its policy of removing Indians to reserved lands and initiated a series of programs to do so. Although not all attempts to separate

Native Americans from their land were successful, none was more disastrous than the Battle of Little Bighorn in 1876.

In 1868, the second Treaty of Fort Laramie gave Indians exclusive rights of the Dakota Territory west of the Missouri River. Still, white miners in search of gold were settling the sacred Dakota land nonetheless. After gold was discovered in the Black Hills of the Dakota Territory in 1874, confrontations between Native Americans and settlers were inevitable. Indians raided the pioneers, but this did not stop white settlement. The government was unwilling to remove the settlers and unable to persuade the Dakotas to sell the land. The U.S. government ultimately reacted by voiding the second Treaty of Fort Laramie to stop the conflict. An order was issued for all Indians to return to their reservations by January 31, 1876, or be deemed hostile. The Sioux and

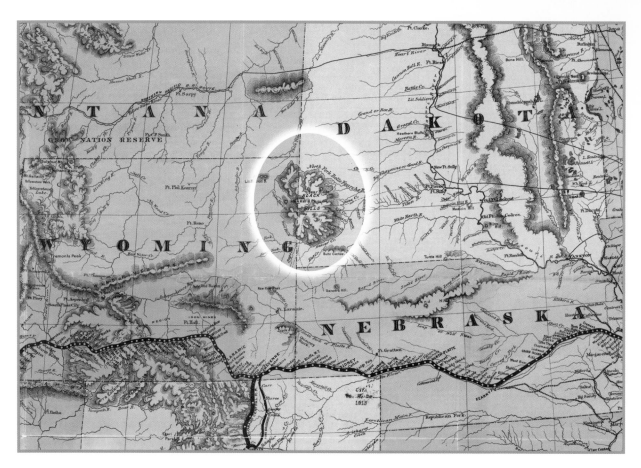

The Black Hills, an area sacred to Native American tribes in the Dakota Territory, is highlighted in this detail of an 1877 map of the western United States. The Black Hills area was closed to white settlers during the 1800s, but after the discovery of gold there in 1874, the agreement to seal off the land to whites was largely ignored by prospectors. Eventually, constant invasions by whites into the area resulted in the Battle of Little Bighorn in 1876.

Cheyenne instead defiantly left their reservations in the Black Hills. They gathered in Montana under the leadership of Chief Sitting Bull to plot the fight to reclaim their land.

Under the command of Brigadier General Alfred H. Terry, the U.S. government hoped to find and kill Sitting Bull's tribes. Terry divided his troops into three divisions. One of the divisions was led by Colonel George Custer, leader of the Seventh Cavalry of the U.S. Army. Custer led his troops to the mouth of the Little Bighorn River where he was to meet the other two divisions.

## Custer's Last Stand

Custer was a brigadier general in the Civil War and later became famous after fighting in the Battle of Little Bighorn ("Custer's Last Stand") on June 25, 1876. Custer discovered Sitting Bull's encampment on the banks of the Little Bighorn River in Montana, and thought he should strike early. Ignoring General Terry's orders to wait, Custer decided instead to wage an attack before alerting the main party. He soon discovered he was severely outnumbered. Surrounded by their enemy, the five companies under Custer's command were slaughtered in less than an hour. Two days later, General Terry, who was expecting to meet Custer and his men alive, instead found their dead bodies. Although it was a commanding victory for Native Americans, their glory was short lived. Public opinion turned against Native Americans and more federal troops were sent into the Black Hills.

Colonel George Armstrong Custer (1839–1876), a general in the United States' Civil War, is pictured along with his cavalry in this drawing by Alfred Rudolph Waud, a Civil War artist. At the time, Custer and his men had burned a wooden area during the siege of Petersburg, Virginia, in October 1864. Although there were no American survivors of the Battle of Little Bighorn, Custer's bitter fight to the end became an enduring legend of the struggle to settle the American West.

Sitting Bull (1831–1890), a war chief and mystic, led the Sioux Nation in resistance against the white invasion of Sioux lands during the 1870s and 1880s. After many years of fighting that took their toll on his health, Sitting Bull eventually died during a gun battle between Native American police agents and other Indians.

When the Dawes Severalty Act was passed in 1887, it became the primary U.S. policy toward the Native Americans until 1930. The idea behind the law was to convince Native Americans to become independent farmers. Indians were granted ownership of up to 160 acres (65 hectares) for each family, with smaller portions given to single tribe members. If they participated, the Native Americans could gain U.S. citizenship and the right to control the land for twenty-five years. Sitting Bull returned from Canada, where he had taken refuge in 1877, to accept lands under the new legislation. The law was another attempt to absorb the Native Americans into the whites' agricultural culture, and it further eroded Native American tradition. Because of the West's drier climate, however, much of the land that wound up in Indian hands was unsuitable for farming.

In the 1880s, the U.S. government forcibly separated Indian children from their families to send them to school, where they received a Christian education. All efforts were made to convert Native Americans to Christianity, a process that whites believed would turn them into "educated and industrious citizens." All Native Americans were granted U.S. citizenship in 1924. It was the final gesture by the federal government to fully integrate them into mainstream America.

L and policy legislation impacted the expansion of the U.S. economy during the latter half of the nineteenth century. After the Civil War ended, the federal government allowed unrestricted use of the land to promote an agricultural economy. Later in the century, when rampant mining, logging, and farming had wounded the American landscape, a conservation movement emerged.

## U.S. Land Policy

Abraham Lincoln signed one of the most important land policies into law in 1862 after the secession of the Southern states. The Homestead Act returned massive holdings of public land to private citizens. This turnover was sorely needed after the loss of contributions by the Southern states to the U.S. economy. The desired effect of the legislation was to convert unused public land into profitable private property. Two hundred and seventy million acres (110 million ha), or 10 percent of the area of the United States, was settled under this law. The Homestead Act gave pioneers a quarter section of land (160 acres [65 ha]) if they built a house, dug a well, plowed 10 acres (4 ha), fenced a specified amount, and actually lived on the plot for five years. The number of cattle in the

Plains states rose from 130,000 to 4.5 million between 1860 and 1880.

There seemed to be an endless supply of timber in the West, and Congress passed another law that encouraged the cutting of trees for profit. The 1878 Timber and Stone Act allowed citizens to buy timber land inexpensively at $2.50 an acre ($6.20 per ha). Lumber and mining companies quickly took advantage of this bargain. It also allowed newly cleared land to be settled. This act ravaged nearly 13.5 million acres (5.5 million ha) of forest, with prices far below market value.

In order for the United States to compete in the global agricultural marketplace, it needed to increase its production while reducing its cost of labor. The Hatch Act was passed in 1887 as an attempt to address that problem. Proposed by Representative William Hatch of Missouri, the law funded the construction of agricultural experiment stations at land grant universities. This act offered funds for agricultural research to improve the production and efficiency of U.S. farming practices. By using student labor, production costs were ultimately reduced.

## National Parks

Despite the trend of using land for farming, some individuals called for the protection of America's landscape. Galen Clark was a New England miner who went to the mountains of California to recuperate from poor respiration. He started a homestead in Wawona, California, that served as a lodge for travelers. Clark was known for his love of Yosemite and was a fierce supporter for the protection of the Yosemite Valley. Because of his extensive lobbying, Lincoln signed the Yosemite Grant on June 30, 1864. The grant deeded the Yosemite Valley and the Mariposa grove of giant sequoias to California, creating the world's first state park. Yosemite State Park is considered the foundation on which national parks were later established, such as Yellowstone National Park in 1872, and Yosemite National Park in 1890.

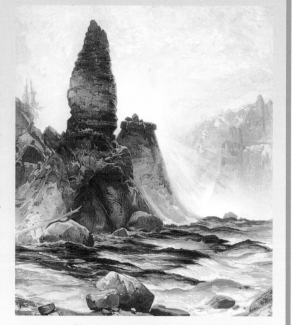

Tower Falls, a waterfall in Yellowstone National Park, is featured in this nineteenth-century print. Yellowstone is known for its thermal springs and geysers, but it also contains thousands of miles of trails, fossil forests, many lakes and streams, and a volcanic "glass" mountain.

# The End of the American Frontier

After the violent confrontations with Native Americans stabilized, additional states joined the Union. On November 2, 1889, North Dakota and South Dakota were admitted on the same day, becoming the thirty-ninth and fortieth states. In the following nine days, Montana and Washington joined as well. Idaho and Wyoming were fast on each other's heels in 1890, bringing the nation to forty-four states. Utah joined the Union in 1896, and with its entry, a new U.S. flag flew with forty-five stars.

In 1890, the U.S. Census Bureau announced the end of the frontier. The days of endless land giveaways started by the Homestead Act had ended. The following year Congress passed the Forest Reserve Act, which empowered the president to create national forests. This environmentalism was possible due largely to the efforts of conservationists. One well-known environmental activist was John Muir, founder of the Sierra Club, which he organized in 1892. Muir decried the expansion of the economy at the expense of the environment. His writings were influential in creating preserves for the Grand Canyon and the Petrified Forest in Arizona and Mount Rainier in Washington State.

In 1902, Congress passed the Newlands Reclamation Act in honor of its chief sponsor, Senator Francis G. Newlands of Nevada. This law set aside proceeds from land sales in sixteen western states as a fund for the development of irrigation projects. The idea was to turn semiarid desert land into farmland through the construction of canals, dams, and hydroelectric projects. The construction of these irrigation projects from 1903 to 1917 created jobs and economic opportunity. Crops such as alfalfa, potatoes, lettuce, celery, and melons grew in what was once Nevada desert.

John Muir (1838–1914), a conservationist and writer, was one of the earliest advocates of environmental issues. A Scottish immigrant, Muir devoted the majority of his life to preserving the wilderness.

# CHAPTER THREE
## Industrial America

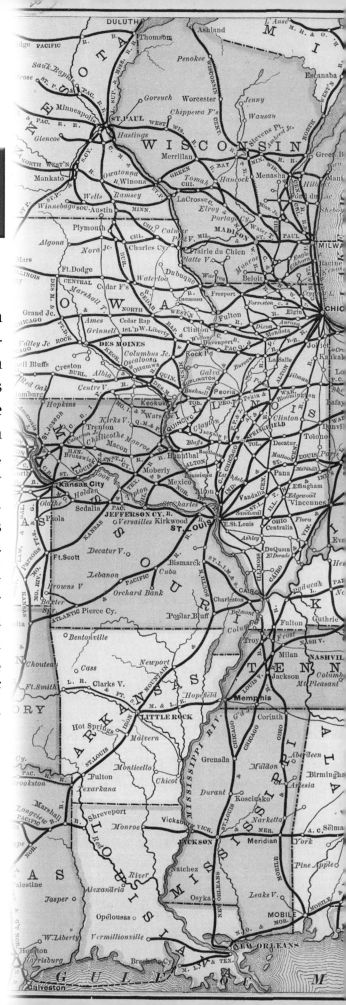

After a long economic depression in the 1870s due to rapid expansionism, the United States began an era of prosperity. This period is referred to as the Gilded Age, a phrase coined by author Mark Twain. Although the country seemed economically sound, Twain believed that it was actually corrupt beneath its "gilded" surface. Employment in manufacturing plants doubled, as industrial jobs lured workers away from family farms. Iron and steel production skyrocketed from 1 million tons annually in 1880 to more than 11 million tons by 1900. The United States was producing a quarter of the world's iron supply by the turn of the century, becoming the world's dominant industrial power.

The eastern half of the United States is shown on this map that features the New York Central and Hudson River Railroad and its connections. Although government subsidies for railroad companies were eliminated in 1870 (Americans voiced dissatisfaction with past relationships they viewed as corrupt), more than 70,000 miles (112,654 km) of rail were laid during the 1880s. Mapmakers for Rand, McNally & Company created this map in 1876.

THE ONLY 4 TRACK RAIL ROAD in the World ALL LAID WITH STEEL RAILS

MAP OF THE New York Central AND Hudson River RAILROAD AND ITS PRINCIPAL CONNECTIONS.

Rand, McNally & Co., Engravers, Chicago.

## The Growth of Industry

The relaxed land policies of the 1860s, which led to the exploitation of natural resources, created the demand for rail transportation. The steel industry profited tremendously from supplying the raw materials needed to connect the nation in a network of railroads.

Technological advances revolutionized the way people lived. America witnessed an age of invention, ignited by the discoveries of Alexander Graham Bell and Thomas Alva Edison. On June 25, 1876, Bell displayed his telephone at Philadelphia's Centennial Exhibition. Ultimately, the invention of the telephone and telegraph allowed businesses to move information quickly, dramatically transforming the speed of communication. Edison's electric lightbulb made him a household name. The banking house of Drexel, Morgan & Company soon organized the Edison Illuminating Company. By 1882, incandescent streetlights illuminated New York City. Electric lighting soon increased productivity, as it allowed working hours to extend past sunset.

Because petroleum was needed to fortify heating and lighting, the petroleum industry also grew rapidly during the Gilded Age. Public utilities were formed to manage the use of trolley cars, telephones, gas, and electricity. The Bessemer process sped up the production of steel, improved its quality, and lowered its price.

On the domestic front, sewing machines now made clothes in hours instead of days, iceboxes and canned goods lessened food spoilage, and ovens came with temperature gauges. As manufacturing

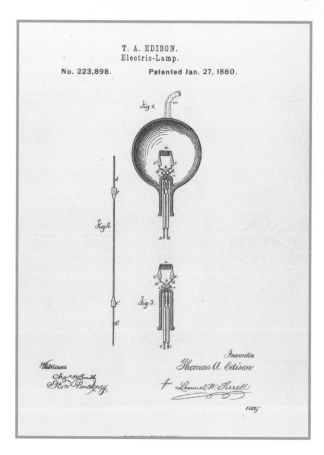

This 1880 document from the U.S. Patent and Trademark Office shows Thomas Alva Edison's (1847–1931) drawing of an incandescent lightbulb. Edison, who was both a scientist and an inventor, is remembered as a true American original. He created some of society's most appreciated appliances, including the phonograph and moving film camera, as well as more than 1,000 other inventions and modifications.

grew, a means of mass distribution was needed to dispense large quantities of products. Chain stores such as the Great Atlantic & Pacific Tea Company developed the standardization of goods in 1859. Department stores, supermarkets, and chain stores ensured consumers the same quality and price of products from store to store.

## Monopolies

Powerful entrepreneurs became the new leaders of American industry, such as John D. Rockefeller in oil, Andrew Carnegie in steel, and tycoon Cornelius Vanderbilt of the railroad industry. At first, these businessmen were seen as heroes who embodied the American dream. That perception gradually shifted as their workers were exploited and competing firms struggled to maintain business against their vast monopolies. Eventually, these "captains of industry," as they were called at that time, were viewed as dishonest, greedy individuals who engaged in unfair business practices to destroy competition. For example, Vanderbilt

The judge in this political cartoon from 1905 is trying to stop journalists from slinging ink at the American oil magnate John D. Rockefeller, boss of Standard Oil. In 1899, Rockefeller had consolidated about forty oil refining companies into one holding company, Standard Oil of New Jersey, which then controlled about 84 percent of oil production in the United States. Rockefeller's expansive wealth and power soon became the subject of great scrutiny, and in 1911, Standard Oil was forced to divide into smaller companies under the Sherman Antitrust Act.

once gave himself a $6 million raise, and $20 million in "watered" stock. Stock watering is defined as the creation of more new shares in a company than is justified by its assets, and falsely inflates its value. When asked by a reporter if the railroads should be run for the public benefit, Vanderbilt said, "[Let] The public be damned."

As the United States became industrialized during the nineteenth century, class distinctions became more obvious. There was a small, wealthy elite who wielded great political and economic power, a middle class composed of professionals and business owners, and a working class of laborers who toiled long hours in factories. The average workday for a laborer in 1890 lasted ten to twelve hours, at an average wage of twelve cents per hour.

A fundamental aspect of American business relied on a laissez-faire capitalist economy. Laissez-faire capitalism is a doctrine that states that a free-market economy functions best when unregulated by the government. However, once wealthy corporations began to abuse the free-market system by manipulating stock prices to their own advantage, there was a need for government intervention. Eventually, the excesses of corporations that banded together to manipulate

entire markets had to be restricted. These like-minded companies became large monopolies that dominated entire industries such as oil refining, sugar processing, and steel production. In 1882, John D. Rockefeller formed the Standard Oil Trust in Ohio. A trust was a new business organization in which a controlling number of shares belonging to competing firms was distributed among a few trustees. These trustees were then able to stop competition between the companies they controlled. The stockholders benefited from receiving larger dividends. When the Ohio courts ruled that trusts violated their state antimonopoly laws, Standard Oil reacted by relocating to New Jersey, where the laws regarding trusts were less restrictive.

## The Sherman Antitrust Act

Standard Oil and the other companies that gained control over particular industries made it necessary for the federal government to get involved in breaking up large monopolies. In doing so, Congress passed the Sherman Antitrust Act of 1890 to dissolve existing trusts and to prohibit the creation new ones. Any trust that was suspected of restricting interstate or foreign commerce through eliminating competition was declared illegal. Individuals

A photographer from the *Chicago Daily News* captured this image in 1907 of lawyers in a Chicago courtroom during the trial that led to the breakup of Rockefeller's Standard Oil monopoly. After the division and subsequent sale of Standard Oil portions, Rockefeller's wealth skyrocketed to $900 million by 1913.

who tried to form trusts would be fined up to $5,000 and subjected to a year in jail. Companies that claimed losses due to trusts could sue for triple damages.

The Sherman Antitrust Act was challenged five years later by the Supreme Court case *United States vs. E.C. Knight* (1895). In this landmark case, it was ruled that E. C. Knight, president of the American Sugar Refining Company, had not violated the Sherman Antitrust Act, although the company controlled nearly 98 percent of sugar refining in the United States. Despite this blow, the federal government invoked the Sherman Antitrust Act against the Standard Oil Company in 1906, amid public outrage. The historic suit against Standard Oil was finally settled in 1911, when its thirty-three corporations were dissolved into six entities. Today, some of these entities are Exxon, Mobile, Amoco, and Chevron.

## CHAPTER FOUR
### Strike, Riot, and Reform

The expansion of industry in the 1800s and 1900s magnified tensions between workers and employers. Workers commonly endured long hours and harsh working conditions without government-sponsored protections. Between 1870 and 1934, the wealthy waged a bitter battle against workers who tried to form unions in order to reform poor working conditions. Despite their efforts, workers continued to organize to gain control over the workplace that had been created by the Industrial Revolution.

## The Organization of Labor

The first national labor organization, the Knights of Labor, was organized in 1869. The Knights wished to incorporate all laborers into a political body regardless of specialization. They were upset by the hardships endured by workers

The business district of Chicago is featured on this panoramic map from 1898. Known as the Windy City because of its unpredictable weather, Chicago became a national center point by 1861, since more railroads met there than in any other city. In 1871, a fire burned 2,000 acres (800 ha) of Chicago and took about 300 lives.

**BIRD'S-EYE VIEW**

Copyright, 1898, by Poole Bros. Chicago, Ill.

# THE BUSINESS DISTRICT OF CHICAGO

during the economic depression of 1873 to 1878. The United States economy failed during these years because of the collapse of railroad investments, which sent the stock market plunging. The Knights were also discouraged by the failure of the Great Railroad Strike of 1877 to improve conditions for rail workers. This strike was important for several reasons; it was the first to be broken by the U.S. military, but it was also the first national strike to draw protesters from coast to coast. This widespread organization indicated how influential a unified labor force could become.

The Knights of Labor gained significant power after Terence Powderly, a railroad worker and the mayor of Scranton, Pennsylvania, took over the organization in 1879. The Knights organized a series of railroad strikes against the Southwest System, Union Pacific, and Wabash railroad companies in 1884. Working together the Knights gained public sympathy and prevented a reduction in wages for workers. Afterward, membership in the Knights of Labor climbed to 700,000 workers nationwide. The Knights then gained enough power to influence Congress to pass a bill prohibiting the immigration of workers who had signed contracts of employment with specific companies.

Terence Powderly (1849–1924) was a machinist, lawyer, and union leader who rose through the ranks of the Knights of Labor in the 1870s. In 1879, he was promoted to Grand Master Workman, the organization's highest position, which he held until 1893. Powderly was also elected as the mayor of Scranton, Pennsylvania, for three consecutive terms from 1878 to 1884.

## Chicago's Haymarket Riot

A nationwide strike of all industrialized workers took place on May 1, 1886, as 340,000 laborers representing 12,000 companies stopped working. The workers demanded that the standard workday be reduced from twelve hours to eight. One of the protests that day was directed against the McCormick Harvesting Machine Company in Chicago. Labor problems at McCormick had been brewing for the past year. On May 3, a rally for former McCormick employees turned into a violent attack on the new hires. Police officers were called in to restore order. Patrolmen beat the strikers with batons and eventually used revolvers. Two strikers were killed, and many more were wounded. In response to the police action, anarchists called for a protest rally in Chicago's Haymarket Square, passing out leaflets that read "Revenge! Workingmen to Arms!" Anarchists wanted

a society based on shared ownership among all groups and individuals. Some anarchists believed in the use of violence to achieve their goals. A crowd of about 3,000 people arrived, including mayor Burly Cater Harrison. After the mayor and about 300 people left, a bomb exploded in the crowd, killing seven policemen and injuring many others. Eight of the anarchists were arrested and convicted of murder, and four were hanged. The governor of Illinois

These illustrations depict Chicago's Haymarket Riot, a violent conflict between police and labor protesters in 1886 that killed seven officers and injured sixty others. The protesters had called for an eight-hour workday during the riot, when an unknown individual detonated a bomb amid the crowd. Eventually, the incident was blamed on the Knights of Labor, though the organization's involvement could never be proven. The portraits are of the fallen officers.

pardoned the remaining three in 1893 for not receiving a fair trial, and the last committed suicide while in jail.

## The Homestead Strike

Although the labor unions were not directly responsible for the riot, the public blamed organized labor for the tragedy. Before long, people

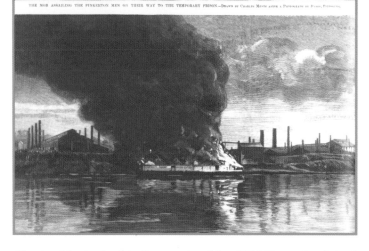

Charles Mente depicts the events of the 1892 Homestead steel strike and riot in these illustrations. The top print depicts the mob assailing the Pinkerton men on their way to prison, and the bottom illustration shows the burning of Pinkerton barges. The Homestead Strike and riot were among several violent eruptions between labor and management that emerged around the United States during the nineteenth century.

associated labor unions with violence. This disgruntled relationship between labor and management only worsened because of events such as the 1892 Homestead Strike, at Andrew Carnegie's steel plant in Homestead, Pennsylvania. The declining value of steel products in the early 1890s led to cost cutting in Carnegie's steel production plant. The general manager of the Homestead plant, Henry C. Frick, tried to ease the problem by reducing wages. His goal was to break the influence of the Amalgamated Association of Iron and Steel Workers, which had many members who worked at the plant. In the spring of 1892, Carnegie instructed Frick to produce as much steel as possible at the plant before June, when the union's contract expired. If the union failed to meet Frick's demands, Carnegie instructed him to shut down the plant until the workers gave up. The Amalgamated Association of Iron and Steel Workers was willing to negotiate its members wages, but it refused to accept the request that it disband. On June 29, while Carnegie was on a vacation in Scotland, Frick shut down the plant and

The Carnegie steel plant in Youngstown, Ohio, is featured in this photograph from 1910. A decade earlier, Andrew Carnegie had sold his enterprise to financier J. P. Morgan for $480 million. Carnegie, who believed that a man should not die without making decent use of his money, donated more than $350 million to various communities and organizations before his death in 1919. Most of the money was spent to help establish more than 2,500 public libraries across the United States.

locked out 3,800 employees. He hired a private police force called the Pinkerton Detective Agency to protect the nonunion workforce he had hired in place of the former organized workers.

Almost the entire town of Homestead flooded to the steel mill, weapons in hand, to meet the Pinkerton ship sailing up the Monongahela River. A battle raged for twelve hours, but the Pinkerton force, who shot at the protesters with Winchester rifles, eventually outgunned Homestead's citizens. By dawn on the following day, the Pinkerton agents raised a white flag. Several men had been killed. The workers accepted the Pinkerton agents' peace offering and let them on shore.

Carnegie was horrified by the violence and alerted the National Guard to control the situation at Frick's request. Homestead was placed under martial law. This is the temporary rule by federal military authority over civilians. By mid-August, the mill was operating again with 1,700 "scabs," so called because they were willing to break the picket line during a strike. An anarchist attempted to assassinate Frick, who responded with a determination to fight the union. Violence against strikebreakers continued until November, when 300 union employees gave in, applied for jobs, and were rehired. Others remained blacklisted. The union was crushed, and Carnegie was free to lower wages, increase the workday to twelve hours, and cut 500 jobs. Regarding the affair, Carnegie wrote, "Oh that Homestead blunder. But it's fading as all events do and we are at work selling steel one pound for a half penny."

## The American Federation of Labor

At the turn of the century, a new organization called the American Federation of Labor (AFL) gained mass appeal despite the violent decade that preceded it. The AFL was a loose federation of local and craft unions that catered exclusively to the skilled trades. Its objectives were to establish better hours, wages, and working conditions. The AFL's weapons—such as boycotts and strikes—were economic rather than political. Samuel Gompers, a New York cigar maker, was a key leader of the AFL from its inception in 1886 until his death in 1924.

## Child Labor

At the turn of the twentieth century, the exploitation of child labor became an alarming national problem. An estimated 1.7 million children were employed by 1900, working as long as sixteen hours daily. Children from poor families were forced to work for pitifully low wages and were denied the opportunity for education.

Writer Harold Faulkner wrote about child labor in his book, *Politics, Reform, and Expansion, 1890–1900*:

> Boys imported from orphan asylums and reformatories to wreck their bodies in the slavery of a glass factory, or of a four-year- old baby toiling until midnight over artificial flowers in a New York tenement—these were conditions that might well shame a civilized people into action.

The industry that first relied on child labor was the clothing manufacturing trade. The Industrial Revolution altered the production of clothing from a cottage industry to a mechanized, factory-based profession. The roots of this transformation originated with the invention of the spinning jenny by Englishman James Hargreaves in the 1760s. Textile mills in New England began using child labor in the early 1800s, as they realized the profits that could be made by employing children rather than adults. Soon many factories employed children. An 1870 census tallied 750,000 underage workers employed in American industry.

By the late 1800s, many textile mills moved from New England to

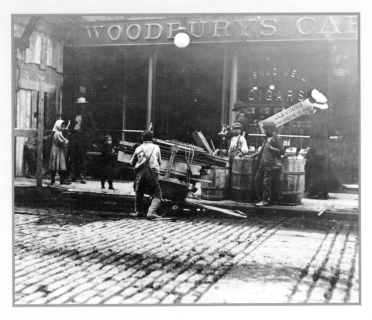

The famous photographer Lewis Wickes Hine captured this image of young boys collecting scrap wood in Boston, Massachusetts, in 1909. At the end of the nineteenth century, many children in the United States took jobs as laborers to help their families make ends meet. The majority of children who worked factory jobs were the sons and daughters of European immigrants.

in heartbreaking detail in his 1890 book, *How the Other Half Lives.*

States such as Massachusetts and Connecticut had had laws prohibiting the employment of children under the age of fifteen since the 1830s, but they were difficult to enforce. Southern states refused to consider such laws in the 1800s. In 1904, a group of social workers, teachers, writers, labor organizers, and fair-minded businessmen organized the National Child Labor Committee, which lobbied Congress to reform child labor laws.

the South. Young men called "breaker boys" were often employed in coal mines. This dangerous work entailed breaking up coal in machines and often caused fatal accidents.

As immigration peaked between 1870 and 1910, the American factory system was fed by an abundance of new workers, mainly immigrants from Europe. Immigrant children were easy prey for the neighborhood industries. Companies that required hand needlework and cigar making found people to work in their tenement apartments or in basements called "sweatshops." Author and photographer Jacob Riis documented the sweatshop system

A prominent member of the committee was Chicago reformer and writer Jane Addams. She moved into an immigrant slum to experience how the Chicago population lived. She also founded a settlement house called Hull House, which was a community center for immigrants.

Most businessmen remained opposed to laws protecting child laborers, but, by 1916, it appeared that the reformers had made progress when Congress passed the Keating-Owens Act. This law barred the interstate shipment of goods produced by child labor. It required factory owners to check the birth

# THE NATIONAL CHILD LABOR COMMITTEE
## WHY?
### TWO MILLION CHILD WORKERS UNDER SIXTEEN YEARS TODAY

## WE WANT THEM TO BE NORMAL MEN AND WOMEN
## YOU WANT THIS TOO
# JOIN
# The National Child Labor Committee

This poster was created in 1910 by Lewis Wickes Hine for the National Child Labor Committee in order to help recruit reformers. The organization was formed in 1904 with the mission to "promote the rights, awareness, dignity, well-being, and education of children and youth as they relate to work and working."

certificates of all job applicants, this time with the threat of jail for owners who violated the law.

Within two years, however, the Supreme Court struck the law down as unconstitutional, because it denied children the "freedom" to work. At that time, the Supreme Court was sympathetic to big business. It wasn't until 1938 that Congress passed the Fair Labor Standards Act, which held that

## Triangle Shirtwaist Factory Fire

Sweatshop conditions and long hours were normal features for factory employees at the turn of the twentieth century, especially for female workers. Factory buildings from this period often had poor ventilation and lacked fire safety regulators such as sprinklers and emergency exits. A heartbreaking example of the occupational hazards people often faced can be seen in the fire that erupted in 1911 at the Triangle Shirtwaist Factory in New York.

Triangle Shirtwaist mainly employed immigrant women, who worked there for about $6 per week assembling women's tailored shirts. Some people were working overtime on March 25 when a fire broke out on the eighth floor. The fire quickly spread to the ninth floor through the Green Street stairwell. Workers rushed to escape through the Washington Street stairwell, but it was locked. Nearly 500 people were trapped in the factory. While many people hurled themselves out windows to their death on the street below, others remained trapped inside and died of burns or suffocation.

In the end, 146 people were killed. Many were outraged by the tragedy. The owners of the factory, Isaac Harris and Max Blanck, were brought to trial for manslaughter, but were acquitted in December 1911. The fire rallied public support for the International Ladies' Garment Workers Union, and led to the creation of the Factory Investigating Commission of 1911.

A group of New York City firemen peers down a hole in the sidewalk in search of victims of the Triangle Shirtwaist Company fire on March 26, 1911, the day after the fire. The tragedy, which was among the worst fires in history, inspired a reform movement to improve safety standards in factories across the United States. Consequently, factory fire codes and child labor laws helped secure a better future for American workers.

children must be at least sixteen years old to work a full-time job.

## Immigration

The insatiable demand for cheap, unskilled labor was fed by a steady stream of immigration at the turn of the twentieth century. Between 1880 and 1920, about 27 million immigrants arrived in the United States. Ethnic neighborhoods soon developed throughout New York and Chicago. Overpopulation in Europe, coupled with rapid industrialization, left many Europeans with dire prospects. Many were forced to abandon their traditional occupations and head to America, which at the time was seen as the land of opportunity.

Industrialists in the United States sought immigrants as low-wage laborers, while steamship owners profited heavily from the scores of people booking passage on transatlantic crossings to America. Some politicians viewed the recent wave of immigration as an opportunity to gain new voters. Powerful political leaders traded jobs and services for votes, creating strong support for their designs. These political groups helped immigrants find jobs on the city payrolls; provided low-cost housing, clothing, food, and schools for their children; and built parks and hospitals in immigrant neighborhoods.

Artist W. A. Rogers created this print called *The Sweatshops* in 1890. It features a group of New York's Lower East Side garment workers. They are carrying bales of cloth to an immigrant tailor so he can sew the pieces together at the rate of fifty cents per hour. This print originally appeared in *Harper's Weekly* on April 26, 1890.

# Tammany Hall

Tammany Hall was a political club in New York City composed of mostly Irish American workers and craftsmen. Tammany men gradually took over the local Democratic Party and turned it into a political "machine." Those who gave money to, or voted for, Tammany politicians were rewarded with jobs, building contracts, or city services.

William "Boss" Tweed, a former volunteer fireman and alderman (assistant to the mayor), became the ringleader of Tammany Hall in 1868, and started an era of extreme corruption. Historians estimate that Tweed drained city finances of between $30 and $200 million through phony legal contracts, kickback schemes, and city work that was never performed.

The Tweed ring lost power in 1871 after investigative efforts by the *New York Times* exposed its corrupt policies. The political cartoons of Thomas Nast also contributed to Tammany's demise, since cartoons were easily understandable to immigrants and others who couldn't read English. Tweed was convicted of forgery and larceny, largely because of the efforts of prosecuting attorney

Hugh Grattan Donnelly created this poster in 1896, twenty-eight years after William "Boss" Tweed became the head of Tammany Hall, the executive committee of the Democratic Party in New York. The dishonesty of Tammany politicians, however, was burned into the minds of New Yorkers even after Tweed and the Tammany "machine" lost power. This poster advertises a play based on the events surrounding Tammany politics during that time, and remains a testament to the widespread interest in the group's corrupt policies.

Samuel J. Tilden, but he only served one year of his twelve-year sentence. He was soon arrested again on other charges, but escaped to Cuba and then to Spain. Tweed was captured in 1876, and died in a U.S. prison two years later.

Between 1870 and 1900, the population of the United States doubled and was about 80 million. About 40 percent of Americans lived in urban areas. Boston, New York, and Philadelphia emerged as urban centers along the Atlantic seaboard, while Chicago became the urban hub of the Midwest. These cities attracted a diverse population that contributed to vibrant economic and cultural climates. Conveniences such as electricity, indoor plumbing, and telephones added to the allure of city living.

## Boston

Boston's growth can be attributed to several factors. Located at the mouth of the Charles River, on an inlet on Massachusetts Bay, Boston had an excellent harbor and became the leading commercial

The routes of the Boston & Woonsocket Railroad in Boston, Massachusetts, are illustrated in this map of the city from 1847. Puritans originally settled Boston in 1630, but like New York, it became increasingly populated by European immigrants during the 1800s. A series of fires crippled the city in 1872, around the same time it was an intellectual center for numerous American writers and poets. Today, Boston is the largest city in New England.

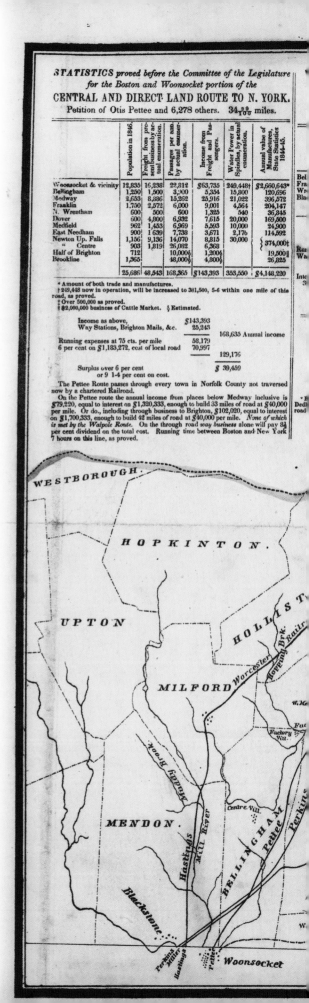

MAP
of the
BOSTON & WOONSOCKET
RAIL ROAD ROUTES
Compiled from the State Map, and the plans
of the different Surveys returned to the joint
Standing Committee on Rail Roads & Canals.
1847.

Lith. of E. W. Bouve. Boston.

center of the original six British colonies. Boston emerged as an intellectual and educational hub with the founding of Harvard College in 1636. In the 1840s, Irish immigrants fleeing the potato famine filled a gap in Boston's workforce, needed for the construction of new roads, canals, and railways. Boston also profited greatly from the Civil War, producing weapons, shoes, blankets, and other goods.

Much like Chicago, Boston was a leader in the abolitionist movement and attracted a steady African American population. Its thriving manufacturing industry also made it a destination for millions of immigrants. Around the turn of the twentieth century, many manufacturing businesses relocated to the South. In their place, service industries such as banking, retailing, and wholesaling prospered in Boston.

## New York

New York emerged at the turn of the twentieth century as the second-largest city in the world with 3.5 million people. The site was discovered in 1609 by Henry Hudson, an English explorer hired by the Dutch to find a faster route to Asia. He quickly saw its potential, befriended the local Lenape Indians, and established a profitable fur-trading business. Dutch colonists came fifteen years later and named the city New Amsterdam.

New York became the largest military base in the world during the American Revolution, when it was overrun by British troops. After America won the war, the city became the first capital of the United States. When the U.S. capital was moved to Washington, D.C., in 1790, New York remained the economic capital of the country.

The early 1800s saw New York turn from a peaceful, rural place to an overcrowded city filled with fires, disease, gangs, crime, and riots. New York rose to the challenge and organized a municipal fire department, utility system, and Central Park, and welcomed the diversity of European immigrants. After the Civil War created massive manufacturing fortunes, New York became home to the greatest concentration of wealth in world history.

This late-nineteenth-century map of New York (including Brooklyn) illustrates the city's network of railroads and principal roadways. Because of its natural harbor and easy access to the Atlantic Ocean, New York quickly became a profit-earning port within a few decades of its discovery by the English explorer Henry Hudson (1565–1611, inset). Hudson explored the Arctic waters of the Canadian north and northeastern United States in search of the Northwest Passage to Asia. Although he died trying to find the mythical water route during his third voyage, the Hudson River was later named in his honor.

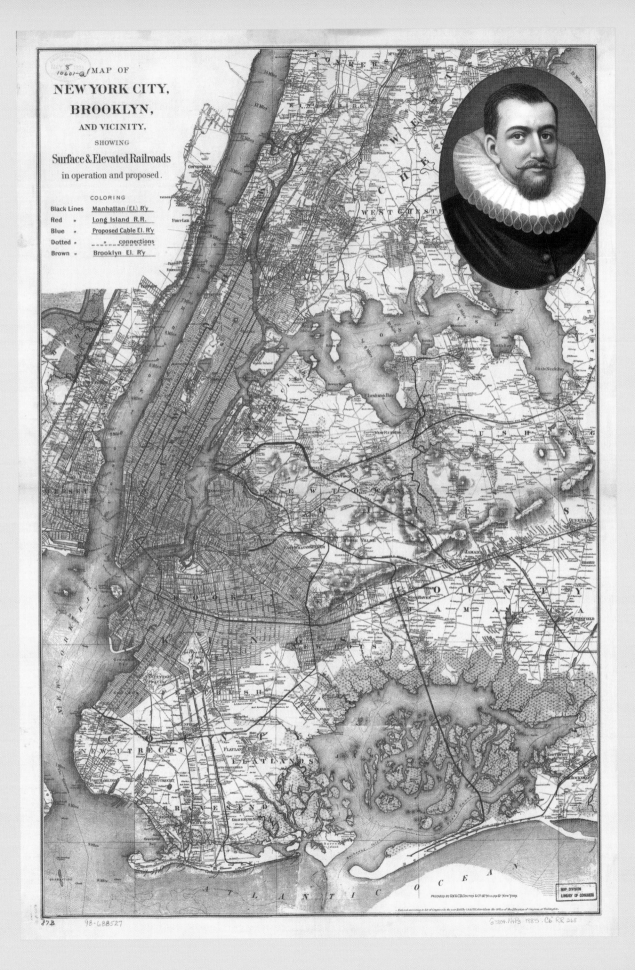

MAP OF
# NEW YORK CITY,
## BROOKLYN,
AND VICINITY,
SHOWING
### Surface & Elevated Railroads
in operation and proposed.

COLORING

Black Lines    Manhattan (El.) R'y
Red     ,,    Long Island R.R.
Blue    ,,    Proposed Cable El. R'y
Dotted  ,,      ,,   connections
Brown  ,,    Brooklyn El. R'y

## Chicago

Chicago was an established fur-trading outpost that revolved around trade with local Native Americans. It evolved into a magnet for young white men seeking a quick profit in the fur trade, and over time, it grew into a trading center during the period of westward expansion.

The federal government purchased land in the Chicago area from the Potawatomi Indians in 1816. Chicago's geographic location between the East Coast and the West

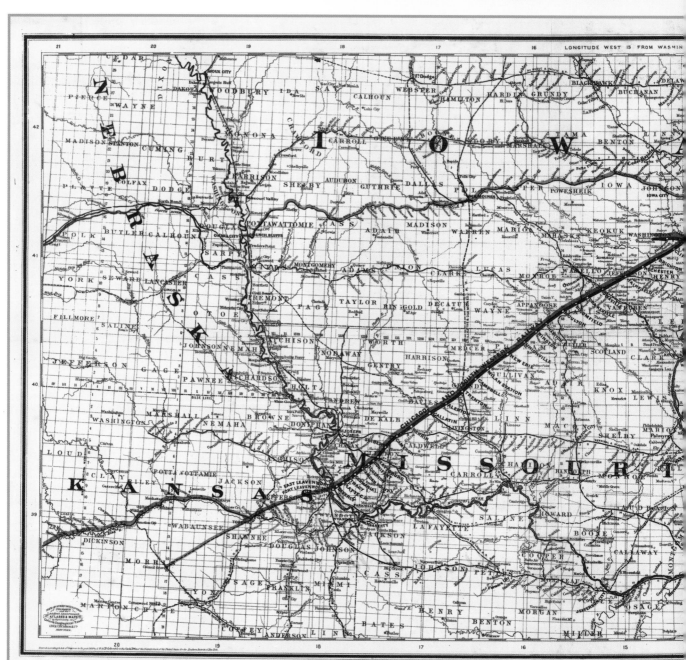

made it a key player in the relationship between agriculture and industry. Its fertile soil and position near Lake Michigan also contributed to its expansion.

By the 1850s, Chicago was an immigrant city that boasted the most culturally diverse population in the country. Since Illinois was an abolitionist state, Chicago became a hub for the Underground Railroad route to Canada. Many African Americans from the South remained in Chicago for this reason.

Skyscrapers began defining Chicago's skyline as improvements in steel, and elevators allowed for taller buildings. In fact, Chicago's Home Insurance Building is thought of as the world's first skyscraper. Built in 1884 as a ten-story structure, it was the first tall building to be supported both inside and out by a fireproof metal frame.

## Philadelphia

Philadelphia was designed in a gridiron pattern by William Penn, who picked its location deliberately as not to displace the local native Lenni-Lenape tribes in the area. Penn founded the city on the principle of religious and political tolerance, and the city soon attracted many Quakers and other religious dissenters.

The eighteenth century was a profitable time for Philadelphia

MAP OF THE
**CHICAGO SOUTHWESTERN RAILWAY**
*AND THE*
**Chicago, Rock Island & Pacific RAILROAD.**
AND THEIR CONNECTIONS.

The routes and connections of Chicago's Southwestern Railway and the Chicago, Rock Island & Pacific Railroad can be traced in this 1869 map. Early in its history, Chicago's railroad system helped establish it as a top supplier of livestock and grain for the United States. In the 1880s, Chicago was a main center of the labor reform movement. Today, the city is the third most populated in the United States with its variety of diverse ethnic neighborhoods.

43

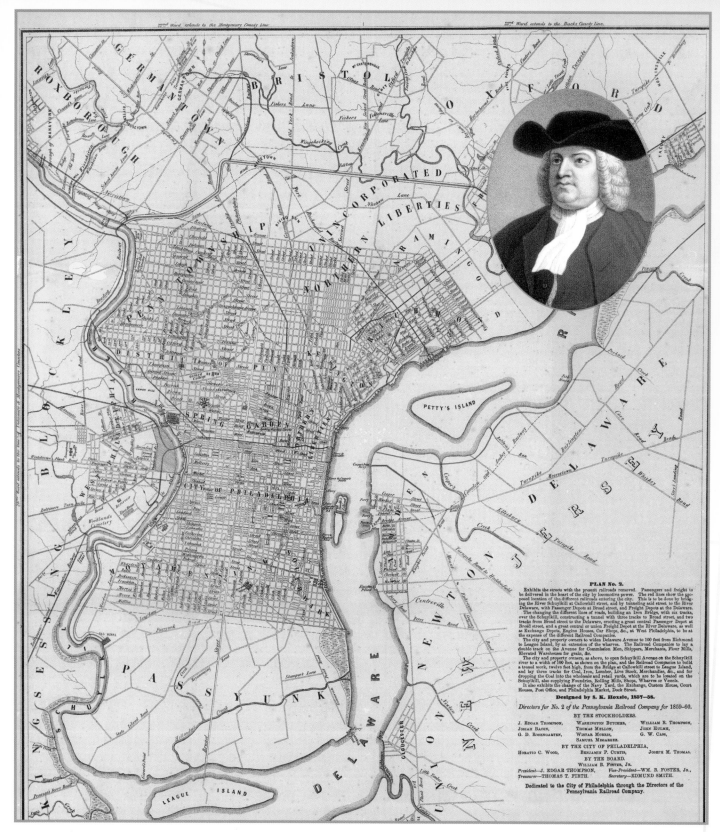

This street map of Philadelphia was drawn in 1858 for the Pennsylvania Railroad Company for the purpose of planning a rail line through the city. Once the nation's capital, Philadelphia has a rich political history. William Penn (1644–1718, *inset*) was an English reformer, colonist, and Quaker who was expelled from Christ Church College of Oxford University in England for being a religious nonconformist. Because of Penn's connections (his father was owed a debt from King Charles II of England), he received a land grant in Pennsylvania and founded the city of Philadelphia.

merchants, who built ships and had a brisk trade in flour and cured meat with the West Indies. The 1800s saw the city turn from a colonial outpost into a gritty metropolis of more than 2 million people. Red-brick row houses sprang up between the Delaware and Schuylkill Rivers, and these outer boroughs were incorporated into Philadelphia in 1854. The creation of the Pennsylvania Railroad in 1846, which tied Philadelphia to Pittsburgh, St. Louis, and Chicago, sealed Philadelphia's fate as major urban hub.

## Civil Engineering

One of the great marvels of civil engineering that changed the face of New York City was the creation of the Brooklyn Bridge. At the time of its creation in 1883, the bridge linked Manhattan to Brooklyn. These two cities were the first- and third-largest U.S. cities, respectively, of the period.

The Brooklyn Bridge was originally conceived in the early 1800s as a solution to overcrowding in lower Manhattan. Building a bridge that linked Brooklyn and Manhattan would allow people and commercial goods to cross the East River quickly, regardless of weather conditions. Before the Brooklyn Bridge was completed, the Atlantic Avenue–Fulton Street Ferry was the fastest crossing between the two boroughs.

Civil engineer John Roebling proposed a suspension bridge

Workers in this illustration from the November 24, 1877, edition of *Harper's Weekly* are razing buildings to make way for the Brooklyn Bridge. Work on the project, the first suspension bridge to use steel cables, was started in 1869. The bridge's designer, John Augustus Roebling, died during an accident during the first phases of the project. Roebling's son Washington took over as chief engineer in his father's place, but soon suffered from caisson disease (the bends) and finished directing the project from his Brooklyn apartment.

across the East River after becoming impatient with the slow pace of crossing by ferry. Roebling planned the minute details of the bridge, envisioning its granite towers and signature steel cables. At first, he was met with little interest in the project. Later, though, Roebling captured the attention of William Kingsley, the publisher of the *Brooklyn Eagle* newspaper. Kingsley brought Roebling's bridge idea to the attention of state senator Henry Murphy, a former Brooklyn mayor. Murphy then drafted a bill to the New York State legislator that allowed a private firm the ability to form the New York Bridge Company. The New York City Council and Army Corps of Engineers approved Roebling's design in June 1869. Unfortunately, that same month, Roebling's foot was crushed on a pier by an incoming ferry while searching for sites to build the bridge's towers and he died. His son Washington took over as the project's chief engineer and saw it through to its completion.

Ground was broken in 1870, and work on the bridge's foundations began. Workers spent their days in a caisson, a large, airtight cylinder, in order to clear away layers of silt underneath the riverbed. It was dangerous and grueling work. Immigrant laborers earned $2.25 per day and were exposed to fires, explosions, and caisson disease (decompression sickness), a condition that affects nitrogen levels in the bloodstream because of changes in

Upon its completion in 1883, the Brooklyn Bridge spanned 1,595 feet (486 m) and was the longest bridge of its kind until the construction of Scotland's Firth of Forth Bridge in 1890. About twenty-seven people lost their lives during the building of the bridge, though exact statistics were not kept at that time. Today, people enjoy the Brooklyn Bridge both by automobile and on foot, as a pedestrian promenade runs its length above the roadway.

air pressure. The bridge towers rose and were then connected by wire and steel suspension cables. The roadway was laid at a height appropriate to accommodate the tallest ships, and elevated railway tracks were planned down the center of the bridge. The outer lanes would be for carriage and horseback riders. In 1883, the Brooklyn Bridge was completed at a cost of about $15 million.

After the bridge opened, improvements in transportation made commuting to Manhattan quicker and easier. Access to the bridge allowed workers to live farther from the city's center, priming the nation for the growth of suburbs. Several streetcar companies even built amusement parks at the end of their streetcar lines in order to sustain profits on weekends. The trolley industry was primarily a private enterprise, but as streets became more congested, city governments recognized the need to intervene.

In the 1890s, the Boston Transit Commission issued bonds to build a tunnel for streetcars beneath Tremont Street in Boston. It recovered its investment by charging rent on the streetcars that used the tunnel, which opened in 1897 and is considered the country's first subway. New York City passed a similar resolution in 1894 to fund transit tunnels using public bonds.

These women are helping a child climb aboard an electric-powered Broadway streetcar in New York City during the summer of 1913. New York City was always at the forefront of public transportation, from the original horse-drawn omnibuses that ran up and down Broadway beginning in 1827, to the innovative electric streetcar of the 1880s. Because so many individuals needed to comb the island of Manhattan on any given day (more than 1 million people lived there by 1880), upgrading public transit systems was always a priority.

However, the New York plan was more ambitious; it planned to use electric trains rather than streetcars to run the entire length of Manhattan and the Bronx. This service became so popular by 1913 that the city called for the expansion of another 123 miles (198 km) of rapid transit, using both private and public funding.

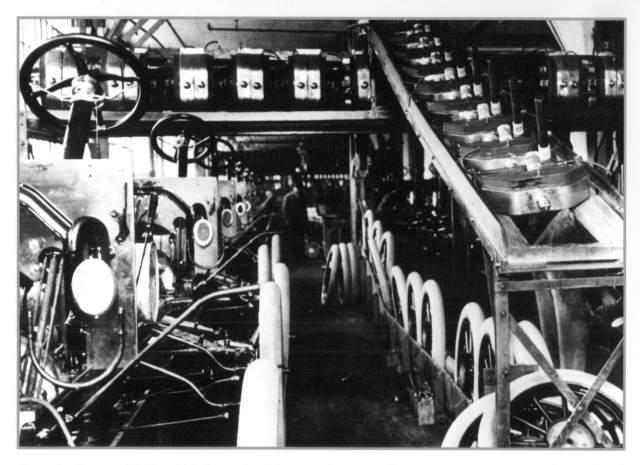

Henry Ford's assembly line at his factory in Highland Park, New York, was a systematic system that produced more cars in less time. Ford, who got the idea for the assembly line after seeing similar methods at a Chicago meatpacking plant, soon became the world's largest car manufacturer. Because the assembly line so drastically cut production time, Ford was also able to reduce the price of each car. These innovative methods resulted in more Americans being able to afford cars.

The demand for gasoline-powered cars grew steadily throughout the 1900s. The American car manufacturer Henry Ford capitalized on this market by inventing a conveyer belt–based assembly line in his factory. Using this method, Ford could produce a Model T Ford in ninety-three minutes. Ford's invention made the mass production of automobiles possible. His goal was to create "a motor car for the great multitude." After 1913, Ford became the world's biggest car manufacturer.

The assembly line soon revolutionized the way all factory-made goods were produced. Eventually, Michigan became the country's center for auto manufacturing. The assembly line was largely a success because of these four principles: interchangeable parts, division of labor, continuous flow of work, and reduced effort.

# CHAPTER SIX
## The Progressive Movement

Although great strides in civil engineering occurred during the nineteenth century, many city dwellers lived in squalor. America's cities converted farmland and single family homes into multi-family dwellings to accommodate the expanding population. From 1870 to 1930, many urban residents wound up in tenement houses, which were densely inhabited apartment buildings.

## Tenements

In tenements, tenants shared communal sinks and bath-rooms, and many rooms were without windows. Several generations of family members often shared a meager space, sometimes along with boarders. Reformers such as Jacob Riis exposed the unhealthy, rat-infested environment of the tenements. Eventually, legislation was passed in 1901 to improve the light, air, and plumbing conditions many tenements lacked. His book, *How the Other Half Lives,* was the first of its kind to use documentary photography. Haunting images along with detailed descriptions profiled the lifestyles of New York's immigrant population.

Another influential book that exposed the plight of the urban working class was Upton Sinclair's 1906 novel *The Jungle.* In 1904, an editor of a Socialist journal

Lewis Wickes Hine (1874–1940) took this photograph of three small boys sitting on the stairs of a Boston tenement in 1909. Hine was trained as a sociologist and first began taking photographs of immigrants in New York's Ellis Island as early as 1905. Many of his later images were of children, and he soon became a documentarian of child laborers in the United States. Some of these images appeared in his 1908 book, *Charities and the Commons.*

commissioned Sinclair to write a story about immigrant workers in the Chicago meatpacking industry. Sinclair described the food contamination and unsanitary conditions that took place at meatpacking plants, as well as the meager living conditions of the workers. President Theodore Roosevelt read *The Jungle* and subsequently ordered an investigation of the meatpacking industry. The Pure Food and Drug Act (1906) and the Meat Inspection Act (1906) came about in response to Sinclair's book. These laws were the first attempts at government regulation of consumer products. Sinclair's writings inspired an era of investigative journalism, which was disapprovingly labeled "muckraking" by Theodore Roosevelt.

## Woodrow Wilson

The second decade of the twentieth century saw a tightening grip by the federal government to regulate

Upton Sinclair (1878–1968), seen here in 1914 with a white suit and black armband, was a significant contributor to America's Progressive movement (c. 1900–1920). Sinclair was an American novelist and muckraker, best remembered for his 1906 book *The Jungle*, an exposé of Chicago's meatpacking industry. Because of the atrocities outlined in *The Jungle*, the U.S. federal government passed the Pure Food and Drug Act and the Meat Inspection Act in 1906.

the economic excesses of the industrial age. Woodrow Wilson secured his term in office under the banner of the New Freedom platform, which proposed to revitalize the American economy by reducing tariffs, strengthening antitrust laws, and reorganizing the American banking and credit systems.

Between 1913 and 1921, Wilson lowered tariffs on hundreds of domestically produced goods with the Underwood Act and created a graduated federal income tax. The Federal Reserve Act of 1913 established the Federal Reserve System of U.S. banks. This act shifted the power from Congress to the Federal

Reserve Bank to produce money and set its value. Wilson also established the Federal Trade Commission in 1914 to prohibit the excesses of unfair business practices. The Sherman Antitrust Act was updated by the Clayton Antitrust Act, which stated that labor unions were not to be considered unlawful organizations that restrained trade. Wilson also introduced legislation banning the use of child labor, limited the work-day of railroad employees to eight

Woodrow Wilson (1856–1924), a governor from New Jersey, became the twenty-eighth president of the United States. He served two consecutive terms that started in 1913 and ended in 1921.Wilson led the United States into World War I (1914–1918), and was responsible for significant legislation during his tenure. These laws included the passage of the Federal Reserve Act and the establishment of the Federal Trade Commission to regulate business practices.

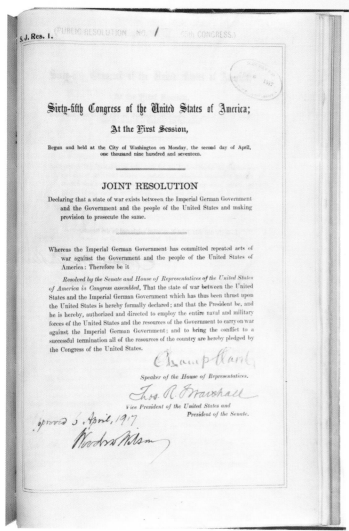

This document is President Wilson's official Declaration of War message to Congress, given on April 2, 1917. Wilson, who had run for office on a policy to keep the United States out of the conflict, urged Congress to approve his decision to enter the war. As part of his argument he said, Americans must "fight for the rights and liberties of small nations" in order to "bring peace and safety to the world itself."

hours, and imposed heavy income taxes on the rich.

Wilson rode into his second term of office on a promise to keep America out of World War I, which erupted in Europe in 1914. But after winning the election of 1916, Wilson felt that he could not remain neutral, and he asked Congress for a Declaration of War against Germany "to make the world safe for democracy." Wilson's decision to enter the conflict was due to Germany's system of authoritarian government and its assault on American trade with Great Britain.

American involvement tipped the balance of power in favor of the Allies, and the Germans signed an armistice in 1918. Wilson met with the leaders of France, Great Britain, and Italy to decide how to redraw the map of Europe. Together the leaders wrote the Treaty of Versailles in 1919, which forced Germany to reduce its army and navy, abandon its air force, and return land to France, Belgium, Denmark, and Poland. Germany also had to abandon its overseas colonies and pay massive war reparations. Some scholars believe that the resentment caused by the harsh conditions of the treaty led to the German aggression that began World War II (1939–1945).

During the 1920s, many young people found themselves disillusioned by their war experiences. They rebelled against prewar conventions they believed were outdated. Women who had worked outside the home because of the labor shortage gained social and economic independence, which they were unwilling to give up after the war ended. Short bobbed haircuts, as well as public drinking and smoking, became the hallmark of the female "flapper" of the 1920s.

## Social Change

The women's suffrage movement, which began in the mid-nineteenth century, saw women gain the right to vote in 1920. The suffragists used tactics such as petitioning, lobbying Congress, marching, and civil disobedience to get their point across. Susan B. Anthony was a key figure in the movement. She registered and voted illegally in the 1872 election and was arrested and fined $100 for "knowingly, wrongfully, and unlawfully voting for a representative to the Congress of the United States."

Not everyone was thrilled with the relaxation of moral standards. The decadence and social change angered many farmers and small-town dwellers. Rural areas became the base for a Christian fundamentalist movement, and residents banded together to preserve

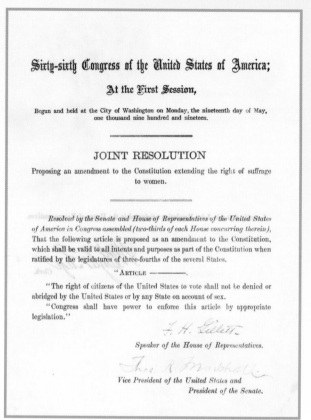

At left, actress Anita Garvin (1907–1994) is pictured in an elaborate beaded flapper outfit from the 1920s. The Jazz Age was the first time that women's fashions and cosmetics were made readily available to all women. Jazz Age icons include writers F. Scott Fitzgerald and Dorothy Parker, comedian Harpo Marx, magician Harry Houdini, and artists Grant Wood and Edward Hopper. At right, the Nineteenth Amendment, which was passed by Congress on June 4, 1919, and ratified on August 18, 1920. It granted women the right to vote after suffragists fought for decades to amend the Constitution. Similar amendments had been introduced as early as 1878, but had failed to win the approval of a majority of members.

what they viewed as decaying moral standards. The Eighteenth Amendment, referred to as Prohibition, banned the manufacture, sale, and transportation of alcohol. Prohibition was considered a huge victory by the millions of devout, Protestant churchgoers who supported it. While alcohol-related health problems appeared to have fallen during Prohibition, nothing could stop the determined from drinking. Drinking establishments called "speakeasies" sprang up, requiring a password from patrons to enter. Women who ordinarily wouldn't be seen in saloons soon found a place in speakeasy society.

In 1925, the fundamentalist movement culminated in what is known as the Scopes Monkey Trial. A biology teacher named John T. Scopes from Dayton, Tennessee, was tried for violating a state law that banned the teaching of the theory of evolution. Scopes was found

John Thomas Scopes (1900–1970, seated second from left) is seen in this 1925 photograph surrounded by his legal staff, which included the famous lawyer Clarence Darrow *(far left)*. In the end, Scopes was found guilty of teaching Charles Darwin's theory of evolution in a Tennessee classroom and was fined $100. The trial was the most sensational of the Jazz Age. Afterward, Scopes fled the region for Chicago, where he received a master's degree in geology.

guilty of violating the law, but the resulting publicity made a mockery of the trial and the town's fundamentalist beliefs.

The early 1920s were known as the Jazz Age, an expressive and freewheeling period of excess and a popular time for speakeasies and jazz music. In the African American community of upper Manhattan, the arts flourished in a movement known as the Harlem Renaissance. Black migration to New York City, Washington, D.C., and Chicago was ignited by the declining Southern economy. This northward migration was considered a spiritual emancipation for many African Americans as it instigated radical intellectual and artistic expression.

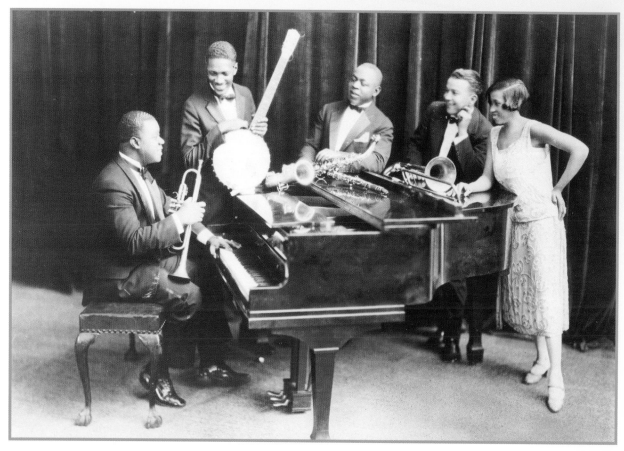

American jazz musician Louis Armstrong (1901–1971) sits at a piano with his band, the Hot Five, in Chicago, Illinois, in 1925. The players, from left to right are: Armstrong holding a trumpet, Johnny St. Cyr with a banjo, Johnny Dodds with a saxophone, Kid Ory with a trombone, and Armstrong's second wife, piano player Lil Hardin.

## Marcus Garvey

Marcus Garvey was an influential leader of the African American community during the Jazz Age. Garvey immigrated to Harlem from Jamaica in 1916. His message promoted the idea that Africa was the spiritual home for all black people. Garvey founded an organization called the Universal Negro Improvement Association (UNIA). This was an organization that planned to unify "all the Negro peoples of the world into one great body and to establish a country and government absolutely on their own."

Garvey's message came at a crucial time. The aftermath of World War I resulted in an economic crisis that furthered racial discrimination, lynching, and poor housing conditions for many African-Americans. By 1919, the UNIA had about 2 million members. Garvey formed the Black Cross Navigation and Trading

Black nationalist leader Marcus Garvey (1887–1940) is pictured in this 1924 photograph. Garvey, originally from Jamaica, spent his early years working to improve conditions for African American workers in Central and South America. By 1914, he had established the Universal Negro Improvement Association (UNIA) in Jamaica, of which a New York City branch would be established in 1917. Garvey's memory and accomplishments remain a testament to his passion toward African American heritage.

Company and purchased two steamships to take African Americans to Africa. After several journeys, the company went bankrupt.

Although Garvey was an honest businessman, his partners engaged in corruption. In 1925, Garvey was convicted of fraud and sentenced to five years in prison. President Calvin Coolidge ended Garvey's sentence after he served half of his term, but he was forced to return to Jamaica. Although the UNIA disappeared by 1930, Garvey established a strong sense of African heritage for African Americans.

## American Suburbs

As the 1920s progressed, increased productivity allowed Americans to experience material comfort. People were working fewer hours and

African American Black Cross nurses march in a parade through New York's Harlem neighborhood in 1922 to raise awareness of the annual convention of the Universal Negro Improvement Association. The organization, which was modeled after the Red Cross, was first established in Philadelphia by key UNIA members such as Henrietta Vinton Davis. The Black Cross was a women's division within UNIA that helped provide public health services to black neighborhoods.

making more money because of improved labor laws and business practices. Available goods such as radios, telephones, refrigerators, and cars, coupled with a credit system that allowed people to buy these items, made life easier. Leisure activities took center stage, and football and baseball became American institutions. Radio serials, tabloid newspapers, and celluloid movies allowed millions of people to share in the world of flappers, speakeasies, and jazz music.

The first automobiles sold to Americans made their debut during the first part of the twentieth century. Soon, hundreds of manufacturing firms were producing vehicles in the United States. Henry Ford's Model T became one of the country's most popular and affordable models. By 1920, Ford had sold more than a million cars. Personal vehicles, like the one shown in this 1925 photograph, opened a new world of travel to people who were otherwise quite isolated.

As automobiles became more widespread, political and economic pressure helped to expand American highways. In the 1920s and 1930s, corporations such as General Motors, Standard Oil, Firestone Rubber, and Mack Truck purchased companies that operated trolleys and trains. The plan was to run these vehicles down until they were unusable, and then create a demand for cars. Public transportation became less accessible and cars became a necessity for suburban life. Americans who had crowded into the cities from the late-nineteenth to early twentieth centuries began to disperse into a suburban sprawl, creating yet a new definition of the American frontier.

# TIMELINE

**1848** The discovery of gold in California starts the gold rush.

**1860** Abraham Lincoln is elected president of the United States.

**1861** The Civil War begins at Fort Sumter in Charleston, South Carolina.

**1862** The Pacific Railway Act initiates the construction of the transcontinental railway.

**1865** President Lincoln is assassinated, the Civil War ends, and the Thirteenth Amendment prohibiting slavery in the United States is passed.

**1867** The Alaska Territory is purchased from Russia.

**1869** The Union Pacific Railway meets the Central Pacific Railway at Promontory Summit, Utah.

**1871** William "Boss" Tweed is exposed in a series of articles in the *New York Times*.

**1876** The Battle of Little Bighorn; Alexander Graham Bell invents the telephone.

**1877** The Great Railroad Strike begins as workers protest a cut in pay.

**1878** The Timber and Stone Act is passed by Congress.

**1879** Thomas Edison invents the electric lightbulb.

**1880** Andrew Carnegie establishes a monopoly in the steel industry.

**1882** John D. Rockefeller forms the Standard Oil Company.

**1883** The Brooklyn Bridge is completed.

**1884** Chicago builds the country's first skyscraper.

**1886** Chicago's Haymarket Riot breaks out; the American Federation of Labor is formed.

**1887** The Dawes Severalty Act and Hatch Act are passed.

**1890** Congress passes the Sherman Antitrust Act.

**1892** The Homestead Strike takes place at Andrew Carnegie's steel plant in Pennsylvania.

**1893** A panic begins a depression following the crash of the New York Stock Market.

**1896** *Plessy v. Ferguson* establishes a "separate but equal" facilities doctrine.

**1901** President William McKinley is assassinated and replaced by Theodore Roosevelt.

**1906** Upton Sinclair's *The Jungle* gives rise to the Pure Food and Drug Act and the Meat Inspection Act.

**1911** The Triangle Shirtwaist Fire kills 146 people in New York City.

**1913** Henry Ford introduces the assembly line.

**1914** World War I breaks out in Europe.

**1916** The Keating-Owen Act stops the shipment of goods produced by child laborers.

**1917** Woodrow Wilson grants a Declaration of War to enter World War I.

**1918** Marcus Garvey organizes his Universal Negro Improvement Association in Harlem.

**1919** The Treaty of Versailles determines the terms of peace in the aftermath of World War I.

**1920** The Nineteenth Amendment to the Constitution grants women the right to vote.

**1924** United States citizenship is granted to all Native Americans.

# GLOSSARY

**abolitionist** An advocate for the elimination of slavery.

**arid** Having insufficient rainfall to support agriculture; dry.

**assembly line** An arrangement of machines and workers in which work passes from operation to operation in a direct line.

**caisson** A watertight chamber used in underwater construction.

**capital** Accumulated wealth used to produce even more wealth.

**conservation** Planned management of public resources.

**dissenter** One who refuses to accept the doctrines of an established church or other organization.

**entrepreneur** One who organizes and assumes the risks of a business enterprise.

**flapper** A young woman of the 1920s who showed freedom from conventional behavior.

**forgery** A copy that is presented as though it were an original, with the intent to deceive.

**frontier** A region that forms the margins of a settled territory.

**fundamentalism** A Protestant religious movement emphasizing the literal interpretation of the Bible.

**Gilded Age** The decade between 1870 and 1880 when the industrialization of America led to corrupt business practices.

**homestead** A settler on public land.

**irrigation** Supplying land with water by artificial means.

**laissez-faire** A doctrine opposing governmental control of economic affairs beyond that needed to ensure peace and property rights.

**larceny** The act of taking something from someone illegally; theft.

**monopoly** Exclusive ownership, usually of a particular industry.

**muckraker** Someone who publicly exposes misconduct of a prominent individual or business.

**petroleum** An oily, flammable liquid obtained from wells drilled in the ground and refined into gasoline.

**Prohibition** The forbidding by law of the sale and manufacture of alcoholic beverages.

**reservation** A tract of land set aside for a particular use. Specifically, the land set aside by the U.S. government for displaced Native Americans.

**settlement house** A community center in which immigrants are taught how to speak and read English and improve the quality of their lives.

**Socialist** Having to do with the Socialist Party, which advocates collective ownership and oversight of the production and distribution of goods.

**suffragist** One who advocates the extension of the vote to women.

**sweatshop** A factory in which workers earn low wages, are employed for long hours, and often work under unhealthy conditions.

**tariff** A charge or tax, particularly on imported goods.

**tenement** A building divided into apartments for rent, usually meeting few standards of safety.

**trust** A group of businesses formed by a legal agreement.

# FOR MORE INFORMATION

National Museum of
American History
Fourteenth Street and Constitution
Avenue, NW
Washington, DC 20013
(202) 633-1000
Web site: http://americanhistory.
si.edu

## Web Sites

Due to the changing nature of Internet links, the Rosen Publishing Group, Inc., has developed an online list of Web sites related to the subject of this book. This site is updated regularly. Please use this link to access the list:

http://www.rosenlinks.com/ushagn/iaga

# FOR FURTHER READING

Clare, John D., ed. *Industrial Revolution*. San Diego: Gulliver Books, 1994.

Fitzgerald, F. Scott. *Tales of the Jazz Age*. Philadelphia: University of Pennsylvania Press, 2003.

Hakim, Joy. *A History of Us: Reconstructing America* (History of Us). New York: Oxford University Press, 2002.

Olson, James S. *Encyclopedia of the Industrial Revolution in America*. Westport, CT: Greenwood Publishing, 2001.

Riis, Jacob A. *How the Other Half Lives – Studies Among the Tenements of New York*. New York: Penguin Books, 1997.

Sinclair, Upton *The Jungle: The Uncensored Original Edition*. Tucson, AZ: See Sharp Press, 2003.

# BIBLIOGRAPHY

Mohl, Raymond A., ed. *The Urban Experience: Themes in American History*. Belmont, CA: Wadsworth Publishing Co., 1973.

Pursell, Carroll W. *The Machine Age in America: A Social History of Technology*. Baltimore: Johns Hopkins University Press, 1995.

Schlesinger, Arthur Meier. *The Rise of the City 1878–1898*. New York: Macmillan Company, 1933.

Smith, Page. *The Rise of Industrial America: A People's History of the Post-Reconstruction Era*. New York: McGraw-Hill, 1984.

Stein, Conrad R. *The Story of Child Labor Laws* (Cornerstones of Freedom). Chicago: Children's Press, 1984.

Summers, Mark Wahlgren. *The Gilded Age: Or, The Hazard of New Functions*. Upper Saddle River, NJ: Prentice Hall, 1996.

# INDEX

# About the Author

Sherri Liberman is a freelance writer who lives in New York City.

# Photo Credits

Cover (background), cover (bottom left), pp. 1 (background), 4–5, 10–11, 14, 20–21, 26–27, 38–39, 41, 42–43, 44 Library of Congress, Geography and Maps Division; cover (top right), pp. 41 (inset), 44 (inset), 48, 56, 59 © Hulton/Archive/Getty Images; pp. 8, 28, 29, 30 © 2003, Photo History, LLC; p. 12 © The Bancroft Library, University of California, Berkeley (BANC PIC 1974.018.6-C); p. 13 President Jackson's Message to Congress "On Indian Removal," December 6, 1830, Records of the United States Senate, 1789–1990, Record Group 46, National Archives; pp. 15, 18, 19, 31, 33, 34, 35, 37, 46, 47, 50, 51, 57 Library of Congress, Prints and Photographs Division; p. 16 © Corbis; p. 22 Records of the Patent and Trademark Office, Record Group 241, National Archives; p. 23 © Culver Pictures, Inc.; p. 25 © *Chicago Daily News* Negatives Collection/Chicago Historical Society; pp. 36, 45 courtesy of Dover Publications "NY in the 19th Century"; p. 52 President Wilson's Declaration of War message to Congress, April 2, 1917, Records of the U.S. Senate, Record Group 46, National Archives; pp. 54 (left), 55 © Bettmann/Corbis; p. 54 (right) Joint Resolution of Congress Proposing a Constitutional Amendment Extending the Right of Suffrage to Women, May 19, 1919, Ratified Amendments, 1795–1992, General Records of the U.S. Government, Record Group 11, National Archives; p. 58 © Underwood and Underwood/Corbis.

**Designer:** Tahara Anderson; **Editor:** Joann Jovinelly